Zebra

by Grace Hansen

Abdo
AFRICAN ANIMALS
Kids

abdopublishing.com

Published by Abdo Kids, a division of ABDO, P.O. Box 398166, Minneapolis, Minnesota 55439.

Copyright © 2018 by Abdo Consulting Group, Inc. International copyrights reserved in all countries. No part of this book may be reproduced in any form without written permission from the publisher.

Printed in the United States of America, North Mankato, Minnesota.

102017

012018

 THIS BOOK CONTAINS RECYCLED MATERIALS

Photo Credits: iStock, Shutterstock

Production Contributors: Teddy Borth, Jennie Forsberg, Grace Hansen

Design Contributors: Dorothy Toth, Laura Mitchell

Publisher's Cataloging in Publication Data

Names: Hansen, Grace, author.

Title: Zebra / by Grace Hansen.

Description: Minneapolis, Minnesota : Abdo Kids, 2018. | Series: African animals |
        Includes glossary, index and online resource (page 24).

Identifiers: LCCN 2017943140 | ISBN 9781532104237 (lib.bdg.) | ISBN 9781532105357 (ebook) |
        ISBN 9781532105913 (Read-to-me ebook)

Subjects: LCSH: Zebras--Juvenile literature. | Zoology--Africa--Juvenile literature.

Classification: DDC 599.665 --dc23

LC record available at https://lccn.loc.gov/2017943140

Table of Contents

Zebra Habitat

Zebras live throughout eastern and southern Africa.

Plains zebras are the most common **species**. They live in large groups in **grasslands** and **semi-deserts**.

7

Zebras spend their days on the move. They are looking for fresh water and grass.

9

Body

Plains zebras weigh between 440 to 990 pounds (200 to 449 kg). They are 3.5 to 5 feet (1.1 to 1.5 m) tall.

Like all zebras, plains zebras are covered in stripes. Their stripes might help protect them. Large **herds** mesh together, making it hard for **predators** to spot just one.

Zebras have large heads. Their mouths are filled with dull teeth. Their teeth help them grind up their food.

Food

Zebras **graze** on grasses, roots, and other plants.

16

Baby Zebras

Baby zebras are called foals.
Females usually have 1 foal every
one to three years. Foals weigh
up to 88 pounds (40 kg) at birth.

18

A foal drinks its mother's milk for a year. After one to four years, young zebras leave their **herds** to join new ones.

More Facts

• Zebras talk to each other using sounds, like barking, braying, and snorting. They also use facial expressions. They show their teeth, and move their ears and eyes.

• A zebra's teeth never stop growing. Its constant chewing helps grind them down.

• No zebra has the same stripes. Scientists think zebras can tell one another apart.

Glossary

grassland – a large area of land covered by grass.

graze – to feed on land covered by grass.

herd – any group of wild animals that travel and feed together.

predator – an animal that hunts other animals for food.

semi-desert – an area that gets little to no rain and is often located between desert and grassland.

species – a group of living things that look alike and make young together.

Index

Abdo Kids ONLINE
FREE! ONLINE MULTIMEDIA RESOURCES

Visit **abdokids.com** and use this code to access crafts, games, videos, and more!

Abdo Kids Code:
AZK4237